I Decided To Live

Rebekah Evans

Published by BooxAi
ISBN: 978-965-578-668-2

Introduction

To truly live, I made the conscious decision to live for myself rather than waiting to die. I realized that the choice was mine alone, and I chose to embrace life fully. Instead of aimlessly rushing through each day, I committed to living each moment as if it were my last, understanding that my life truly depended on it.

I recognized the immense power of words, knowing that they held the ability to bring both life and death. It required no more energy to be negative than it did to be positive. Reflecting on my journey thus far, I faced two options: to become bitter and complain, or to become better despite the challenges, trials, and tribulations. Have you ever felt like you were slowly dying while merely surviving day by day?

I certainly have, and this is the story of how I chose to embrace a life of everlasting freedom, refusing to simply exist as a mere statistic or a worn-out tool in this world.

Rebekah Evans

Chapter 1

Who I was

In my early years, I possessed a combination of innocence, hopefulness, and inquisitiveness, yet I also carried a sense of despair and an intense desire to find a sense of belonging for almost three decades of my existence. My upbringing was under the care of my adoptive guardian, who did her best with limited resources. However, our stability was always uncertain, whether it was finding a place to live due to frequent evictions, giving up soccer in college to work multiple part-time jobs to pay for school, or stepping away from church to focus on my relationship with God. These different paths my guardian and I took in life felt overwhelming as if I was struggling to stay afloat. Despite appearing as a 'good-looking Christian' externally, I feared being knocked down by life's challenges.

I learned at a young age that a little ball called a soccer ball became my best friend for most of my life. I mean let's all face it, it was no "Wilson" from the movie called Outcast, but the ball wouldn't yell or scream at you, so it's a win-win. A.K.A., stay tuned for the next episode called, "I think I found my friend".

However, I had experienced various paths in life; some were challenging, and others were not, but now was the moment to set aside everything and confront what I would call 'the unfamiliar', yet God would call 'the known'. It might not have been familiar for me to move ten times in two years of high school, it might not have been familiar for me to suddenly quit playing soccer and take on five jobs to pay for college, and it certainly was unfamiliar to discover my true identity in this life as I strive to stand on my own, live independently, and be a homeowner while working two full-time jobs and residing in a mobile home.

From an early age, I possessed an innate ability to establish connections with individuals from diverse backgrounds and walks of life. Whether it was in educational institutions, places of worship, social establishments, supermarkets, or random locations in Southern California, I was recognized by everyone. For example, I would unexpectedly come across a former neighbor in the parking lot of Disneyland or encounter a previous pastor at a garbage disposal site in Big Bear before going to work the following day. These encounters made me realize the profound interconnectedness of our world.

I was perceived as having it all together, but in reality, I felt like I was failing in everything except for pleasing others and sacrificing myself to meet their expectations. If you needed a ride home from the beach because you had too much to drink, I would be there to rescue you. If you found yourself stranded at Walmart in scorching heat for hours, I would offer you my car, even if I needed it myself. I realized that I had become a savior to others, but I had neglected to introduce them to the true Savior who can save us all. I finally understood that I was depleting myself and not achieving anything meaningful in my life, whether it was at school, church, with my guardian, or while doing ministry on the streets.

I obtained my degree in Kinesiology, but I failed to pass a state examination that would have allowed me to pursue teaching positions in other schools. I sought leadership roles in churches, but when I confronted myself in the mirror, I realized I was clueless about how to navigate this life. Overwhelmed by the anxieties that the world presents, despite the Bible's teachings to not be anxious about anything, I struggled to understand how to truly embody these principles due to my weak or non-existent relationship with God. I attempted to live with my Guardian, but we constantly clashed, and she would repeatedly evict me from the house. I engaged in ministry work with the homeless on the streets, yet every time I prayed for them to change their ways, they remained stuck in their old beliefs, circumstances, habits, and routines regardless of the time that had passed.

In my awareness, I consistently found myself falling short, whether it was through the words of others or my thoughts. The most heartbreaking part was that I believed the lie that I was inferior. In reality, all I needed to do was stay focused and not be indecisive while moving forward, avoiding distractions, and not dwelling on the past. In the scriptures, it is written that when Lot's wife looked back, she turned into a pillar of salt. Lot's wife was torn between her old life and the unknown future, and her hesitation cost her life. Similarly, God was calling me to leave behind what was familiar and embark on a journey into the unfamiliar with Him. In doing so, I would need to let go of everything and keep my gaze fixed on what lies ahead.

Let's continue. Not only was I brought up to keep my personal and private matters to myself, but I also lacked self-confidence and didn't know who I truly was. How strange is that? Consequently, I allowed the chaos of my life to revolve around me because I didn't want others to see the true extent of the difficulties I faced. Even though I claimed to follow Christ, I became conflicted and uncertain about the path that led me to this life. Jesus stated in His teachings that 'those who have not seen me will do great things,' yet I found myself behaving like Jonah, running in the opposite direction towards darkness. I had been chosen and blessed, but I chose not to embrace my purpose and follow God's will because deep down, I was afraid, insecure, undervalued, and intimidated. I was afraid to uncover the layers of my identity and family history. I was unwilling to live for myself and instead lived in the shadows of how others perceived me, which only devalued me further. As I pursued personal growth, the lies and criticisms within my family mocked me and disregarded my potential. I was intimidated by the idea of leaving behind the humiliation of my past and stepping into the future that our Heavenly Father had always envisioned for me - a future of purity and righteousness. I saw myself as an elephant, restrained for so long, but even when the restraints were removed, I couldn't embrace a life of freedom and abundance due to the lingering voices and falsehoods from my past.

Furthermore, I was the individual who remained silent and refrained from divulging any information, keeping hidden truths to myself. Secrets such as not disclosing that we had contacted the authorities regarding the erratic behavior of your biological mother, who had been yelling and brandishing a knife at us. Another secret is that your brother, who had not been raised with you and had just been released from juvenile detention, had perpetrated abuse against you shortly after your biological mother's passing. These were not merely the words of others, but they were the words that I consciously chose to accept and heed both before and after my conversion to Christianity. I would put on a facade for the churchgoers, knowing that they did not reside with me. Observing someone for a mere fifteen seconds is one thing, but living with them for three hundred and sixty-five days is an entirely different experience. Few truly understood that as I grew older, I developed coping mechanisms to suppress my emotions in an unhealthy manner. Consequently, I experienced excessive stress, entertained suicidal thoughts, succumbed to depression, and grappled with intense anxiety by the age of fifteen.

Moreover, I was among those who professed a deep affection for the concept of the Divine, yet never truly embraced the opportunity to intimately know our Heavenly Father. If I lacked genuine and meaningful connections with others throughout my entire life, how could I possibly cultivate a personal bond with an unseen and unheard God? In close relationships, you can openly share your true emotions when someone asks how you are doing. You can honestly say that you need help to prevent losing your home, dealing with car troubles, and managing financial difficulties. This level of trust is based on a genuine relationship where you believe the person will respect your privacy.

A connection that appears, sounds, and is intimate with one another signifies that both individuals have spent time with one another not on a surface level but on a profound level. The level that reveals what was concealed in darkness and brings it into the light. I needed to recognize that I lacked things in my relationship with God because I did not ask for them. I believed that if God provides for the birds and the fish, then surely, He can provide for me as His child. However, did I genuinely have faith in that statement, or did I believe the lies of my enemies and adversaries who said I would never measure up? Or perhaps, it was my lack of trust in my own beliefs all along? Consequently, I chose to live my life for myself and consume the teachings of the Word, rather than fully embracing and living them out. I wasn't taking responsibility for what I professed because I was indecisive. God was urging me towards a radical and unwavering faith that would ultimately transform my mindset, actions, and the nourishment my soul receives.

In my experience, I always wore a facade to appear virtuous. By doing so, I constructed an illusion of being multifaceted, playing various roles and holding numerous titles. However, deep down, I felt like a decaying body slowly fading away. This feeling persisted even after I professed my faith in Jesus as my Savior. As I accumulated different positions within the church and served as a leader for over ten years, I came to realize that it was all meaningless. Even though my presence in the church positively impacted and guided others toward Christ, it seemed that my personal life lacked any significant growth. Nonetheless, God was always in control, even when I failed to recognize His presence. Many unfair events unfolded in my life, but one thing remained constant - my need for a genuine and reverent relationship with God. I desired a relationship that went beyond mere lip service and produced tangible results. In essence, I longed for a relationship that brought abundant life. To achieve this, I understood that I had to take a leap of faith into the unknown.

Chapter 2

Awakening Signals

Now at the age of twenty-eight, I begin to contemplate and inquire. Such as, why am I making no progress in life? There was something just not connecting. I grew up observing my friends acquire cars while we were selling our vehicles to make payments on all these bills. Then I was fortunate enough to receive cars, but every month these cars would break down on me and I would end up broke every time I received a paycheck. I was able to make a down payment on a vehicle to improve my credit to eventually purchase a home on land; all the while, unaware that this vehicle would soon become my literal home on wheels while working two full-time jobs. Feeling completely exhausted and worn-out repeatedly, I then questioned myself, 'was I simply existing in this life to be a tool or a statistic for the remainder of my life'? If so, why was I the one who dealt with these sets of circumstances? Was I just being taught poverty through this generational curse that I had? One way or another, I fervently pleaded with God to rescue me. Unbeknownst to me at the time, God was guiding me through these tests and trials. In other words, these were the challenges and hardships in life that would shape me into the woman that God intended me to become.

I then pondered. Let's start all over again, beginning at the age of five. I entered school without any idea of where to go for classes and struggled to grasp the concept of learning numbers in elementary school. The school diagnosed me with a learning disability, while my guardian believed I was simply lazy. Throughout elementary school, I tried to understand how my brain worked and questioned why I excelled in understanding people and life problems but struggled with solving word problems in class. Not only was I terrible with numbers, but I also struggled with grammar and comprehension throughout my school years. So why am I writing this book now, considering all these 'issues' I had? Well, let's return to the story.

Growing up in a home where I was never able to meet my guardians' high standards of cleanliness, I constantly faced criticism and was yelled at for not being perfect. It's no wonder that at the age of five, I found peace in my soccer ball, which became my closest companion. I internalized the false belief that I was unintelligent or foolish, despite having a name (Rebekah) that I should have identified with instead of those lies. School was a constant struggle, with low grades and frequent visits to the office for extra help. Most days, I eagerly awaited the end of classes so I could grab my soccer ball (my best friend) and head to practice, even arriving early. These were the formative years of elementary and junior high that led me into high school.

Throughout high school, I faced challenges in passing my classes due to a learning disability. Although I was placed in regular classes, I struggled with severe testing anxiety. This caused me to feel embarrassed about needing extra time for tests and being labeled as special needs. Despite these difficulties, I found solace in making friends, excelling in soccer, and becoming more involved in church. However, I became aware that it was unfair for me to receive hints and answers during tests while my classmates did not have the same advantage. This realization led me to decide to transition from Special Ed to General Ed classes without any aid. It was a daunting task, but I dedicated myself to completing all assignments and seeking extra credit. While I still struggled to pass tests, I managed to graduate from high school. I will always remember the discouraging words from the disabilities department, suggesting that I may never succeed in college. These words filled me with self-doubt and made me question my intelligence. Despite the temptation to rely on aids for test answers, I refused to let that be my path. I chose to separate myself from adapted education and fully embrace general education.

Throughout my high school years, I faced numerous challenges, including moving ten times in just two years. These moves were incredibly difficult, but with the help of God's goodness, grace, and mercy, I managed to navigate through them and transition to the next phase of my life. As I embarked on my journey in Christianity, dealing with constant relocations, the loss of my biological mother, enduring abuse from my brother in silence for eight years, and trying to understand the dynamics of living with my guardian, I found it hard to cultivate a personal relationship with God. I struggled to form personal connections with anyone, including myself. Growing up, I was taught not to show weakness, so I would put on a facade of having everything under control and appearing fine on the outside. However, internally, by the age of sixteen, I was filled with doubt, low self-esteem, and a sense of worthlessness. The only place where I felt confident was on the soccer field. To escape from these negative feelings, I became heavily involved in church activities. Unfortunately, in doing so, I unintentionally neglected to nurture a personal relationship with our Heavenly Father.

I continually entered and exited my guardian's life, but always felt inadequate and like I was constantly missing the mark. So, I decided to follow my guardian's strong suggestion and seek counseling to get my life on track. However, I soon realized that I was just wasting money by discussing my fleeting emotions and surface-level issues. I needed guidance that would propel me forward, not only in my relationship with my guardian but also in my own life. I had to figure out how to navigate life after college without a permanent place to live, relying on sporadic room rentals. I was trying to save money but also had to deal with car repairs for the vehicle I had given to my guardian. I wanted to find a way to earn more money and achieve stability, but my current job didn't provide enough income throughout the year. Additionally, I discovered that I wasn't qualified for higher-paying jobs due to a lack of experience. How could I find answers to truly living my life instead of merely surviving day by day? Surface-level conversations with my therapist and psychologist involved briefly explaining the challenging circumstances of my birth and the negative impact of other people's actions on my life. For instance, my biological parents were unfit to raise children and irresponsibly had multiple pregnancies. I happened to be one of those children born into a chaotic world in 1993.

I always struggled to find the guidance I needed to progress in my chaotic life. Instead of seeking help from counselors and therapists, I initially turned to God, praying for a way out of the situation He was already guiding me through. While I was still clinging to my old life and feeling overwhelmed, God was calling me back to Him. My relationship with my guardian became strained, so I stopped seeking answers from them. The church became my sanctuary, where I could be left in peace. However, I eventually realized that I needed to move forward and leave the past behind. The professionals I sought help from ultimately determined that I was mentally healthy and had no underlying issues. It became apparent that even these experts had their problems, reminding me that we are all human.

So, 'how are you doing physically?', one may ask, since I grew up as a dedicated athlete who never took care of her body by going to the chiropractor. Well, let me tell you. After quitting soccer at the age of twenty-five at Azusa Pacific University and taking on five part-time jobs to pay my tuition and get through school, my physical body went through so much stress that I had stomach ulcers, arthritis in my back due to biking sixty miles every week, and a worn-out nervous system that almost landed me in the hospital just before graduating college from exhaustion. Remember the old saying is, 'No pain, no gain.' I thought to myself then, okay God, it's time for you to guide me through this too.

Furthermore, I was given a plethora of lab results that were incomprehensible to me unless I resorted to searching for their meanings online after visiting the doctors. (By the way, it's worth noting that Google doesn't always provide the most accurate answers, despite what people may say.) On top of the diagnoses given by others, the doctors themselves concluded, 'There is nothing wrong with you. Go home, you're perfectly fine. Just focus on eating healthier and exercising more.' They delivered this message with smiles on their faces and compassionate eyes, but deep down, I knew there had to be something still amiss. Are they joking? How could I possibly exercise more when I can barely stand up during my day job because I've been working all night at my second job (juggling two full-time jobs for a while)? And how can I improve my diet when I don't have a place to call home and cook meals in a kitchen, as I live out of my vehicle? Besides, how can I dine out knowing that almost every establishment serves food containing GMOs?

So, what else could I do, or who should I talk to? Well, isn't God that great a healer? Hmmmm, I wondered 'as a believer', maybe I should seek His guidance through prayer, and He'll bring about miraculous healing from within. After all, Jesus performed numerous healings, right? Again, I found myself consumed with praying to God for superficial matters, without truly nurturing my relationship with Him. It didn't even occur to me that a woman in the Bible was instantly healed because of her faith in Christ. So, where was my faith? Was I placing it in God, trusting that He will make a way even when it seems impossible, or was I simply accepting and assuming that this was my fate for the rest of my life? I knew I had strong faith, but how was I utilizing it? Was I using it to oppose God's plans for my life? Or was I using it to submit and surrender to God's authority throughout my life? Deep down, I knew that I was treating God as a genie, expecting miracles on demand, while still claiming to be a follower of Christ and encouraging others to trust in God during their struggles. My faith was constantly being tested, and I wasn't ready to fully trust God because I kept making mistakes and falling short. I didn't know how to have genuine and vulnerable prayers, instead of just surface-level requests, because I was afraid of losing everything and taking up my cross while putting in the necessary effort. I put in the effort by not worrying about anything but surrendering everything through prayer and presenting my requests to God. The effort of laying down everything to follow His will and remain loyal to Him. The effort of sacrificing my own life in response to His sacrifice for me, when He didn't have to. He was the one who could have called upon a legion of angels to save Him from the cross. This is and continues to be the kind of commitment and sacrifice that God has called me to. However, there are often traditions and conditions that come into play.

Much of it for me was influenced by my upbringing. I was raised to stay silent, punished without knowing why, and even had a memorable incident involving a broken wooden spoon. As a result, I became adept at engaging in superficial conversations without truly knowing the people around me as a defense mechanism. I would always prioritize others' needs, allowing them to feel good while no one bothered to ask about my well-being because I appeared fine on the surface. Our conversations revolved around topics like education, religion, and employment. I preferred to let others do the talking, remaining quiet and avoiding delving into my own complicated life. Within the church, I spent over ten years speaking to young people about the essence of Jesus, helping them understand His significance. However, I failed to cultivate a personal relationship with Jesus early on. While I held a leadership role in the church and shared stories about God from the Bible, I never truly practiced living out a daily personal relationship with God outside of church.

In my relationship with God, things were different. He knows every detail about me, from the strands of hair on my head to the way I was formed in my mother's womb. He was drawing me into a deep and intimate connection with Him. It was a relationship where we delved into the messy realities of life, not knowing that we would soon embark on a journey into the unknown, which He called familiar. It required sacrificing everything, surrendering to God, and leaving behind all that I held dear. Just like Jesus told the rich young ruler to let go of everything and follow Him. That kind of relationship. For most of my life, I was merely surviving, not truly living. I believed that I had already given up everything to provide for my guardian and myself. I couldn't afford to let go and follow Jesus, fearing that we would end up homeless again. But I was always seeking Him, like searching for hidden treasure every day. God knew that I would reach a breaking point soon, and He never left my side, even when people abandoned me, doubts crept in, and I lost my job due to the pandemic. God was always there, working out His plan.

Now almost approaching thirty years old I began to contemplate my spiritual journey and how I had strayed from God and His teachings. I had been reading and learning about faith in the Bible, but I had not been applying it to my own life. I questioned why Christians, including myself, read about these faithful individuals in the Bible but fail to live out our own lives with the same level of faith. I wondered why, as a professed follower of Christ, I was not living in a way that reflected my beliefs. I realized that it is not enough to simply hear and read the word of God; we must also put it into action. I questioned why, if we are told that we are more than conquerors, I often felt like a failure. If I claim to follow a powerful and all-knowing God, why do I feel inadequate and insufficient? Despite attending church, listening to sermons, and engaging with Christian media, I still saw myself as a failure and disconnected from my purpose. I longed to bear fruit and live a meaningful life, rather than just existing. I desired to belong to God's kingdom as His heir, even if I felt estranged from my own family.

Calmly, He continued to call me closer to His family. At a crossroads in my life, I questioned the need for a stable foundation, whether I identified as a Christian or not. After extensive searching, I discovered that our heavenly Father was the one who had raised me in the truth. It is written in the scriptures that even when your earthly parents abandon you, He is there to guide and teach you in the ways of God. This realization was a definitive moment for me, inspiring me to start truly living my life instead of merely surviving and clinging to hopelessness.

Chapter 3

My Current Identity

In the realm of spirituality, I discovered that my connection with the Divine was just beginning. I realized that I am chosen and loved by God, who created me. I am empowered and destined to carry out my purpose. I have authority over challenges and can overcome any obstacles. This realization fills me with enthusiasm and motivates me to embrace each new day with excitement. Let's embark on this journey together! Well, so I thought.

Although those statements may be accurate, I was in for a shocking realization. So, you're saying that God specifically selected this individual as His child, even though for most of my life I have felt insignificant and struggled to endure my existence on this forsaken earth? Are you also implying that I am divinely chosen and obligated to bear a burden? Whose burden are we referring to, by the way? 'Cast out the Legion? I can't even get rid of the GMOs in the Popeyes chicken I eat every day! I mean, come on, is that even real chicken? How can I do this if I grew up without guidance, lacking a personal connection with God or anyone else, not even knowing who I am? From a young age, I was taught to just go to school, forget about soccer, get a job, and make money, just to survive and repeat the cycle.

In the past, when I was a troubled teenager, my guardian didn't know how to handle me. She was dealing with her struggles, and in her desperation, she turned to the church for help. Looking back, I realize that it's not just about having a village to raise a child, but rather having the right people who are capable of nurturing and guiding them. It's not enough to have someone who appears to be good on the outside but is abusive or neglectful when no one is watching. It's crucial to have a solid parental unit or at least one person who can provide a wholesome upbringing. I used to believe that people in the church were perfect and faultless, but I've come to understand that everyone falls short. It is through the Spirit of God that we can find true guidance and discernment, distinguishing His voice from the noise of the world.

During my upbringing, there was a significant turning point when my guardian entrusted me to devout individuals from the Church. Sadly, my biological mother passed away shortly after meeting my father and brother. Additionally, my brother briefly stayed with us but ended up mistreating me before leaving. To make matters worse, this all happened just before the 2008 market crash, resulting in us losing everything. As I mentioned earlier, my guardian dropped me off at the church hoping that I would find solace in Jesus due to the overwhelming chaos in our lives. Surprisingly, her wish came true! When I was about to turn sixteen, I openly professed my faith in Jesus as my Lord and Savior, although internally I struggled with understanding how to truly live it out.

I believe I spontaneously became a Christian and left it at that. I felt joyful and elated, but I struggled to put it into words for God or anyone else. It took me eight years to talk about what my brother had done, and during that time, I found solace in the church building without realizing that God was already dwelling within me. I would hear about abiding with God, but I was never taught that having a relationship with Him could be so intimate. Growing up without this understanding made it confusing for me. So, I sought comfort and belonging in the church community, but I still felt lost without a constant connection to God. The people in the church became like family to me, and I often turned to them for support instead of talking directly to God as His child.

I was well-known within the church community. After high school, I became a leader and got involved in recovery and homeless ministries. The journey of life reveals different levels of truth, but the spirit is the ultimate truth. There are no doubts or reservations. When you connect with God, He will reveal the truth about your purpose and guide you out of darkness into the light. God resides within all of us. Despite all this, I still lacked a personal relationship with God, the kind that preachers often talk about. Instead, I focused on seeking approval from others due to feeling rejected at home and struggling with thoughts of failure in school. I didn't fully trust in the Lord and relied on my understanding. I wore masks and projected an illusion of being a faithful Christian, but I wasn't truly living out my faith in my personal life. I was a hearer of the word, but not a doer. I performed acts of service and worshiped in public but neglected my relationship with God. It became a habit during the early stages of my spiritual journey. Looking back, it seems foolish to have trusted in signal lights, chairs, and technology more than the One who created me. Google couldn't provide the real and unfiltered answers I needed. I didn't give God the time and open heart He deserved. It took years for me to slow down and truly listen for His answers to the questions that plagued me: why did I lose my biological mother, why was I given a family that lacked compassion, and why did I survive abuse? The answers didn't come immediately; it required a change in my heart posture and a willingness to listen.

I fell in love with the concept of being a Christian; however, if I grew up without any guidance on how to develop a personal connection with God and everyone saw me as someone who had it all figured out, then how can I possibly establish a relationship with God? I had no idea where to begin. I started engaging in various religious activities that benefited the Church, but there was no real spiritual growth. In other words, I lacked an authentic relationship with God because most of my upbringing focused on accomplishing tasks without any room for emotions or feelings. I had no space for meaningful connections. Some might say I was too straightforward. I lacked a filter and had no outlet to express my emotions and feelings. For instance, during my sophomore and junior years of high school, I moved ten times. I vividly remember hastily packing up our belongings within thirty minutes to move to the next house. I also recall the first time we moved without any electricity in the house and a police officer warning us to vacate the premises by a certain time when I was just sixteen. Another time, we were kicked out of someone else's house simply because we didn't adhere to the owner's rules shortly after starting college. My time was mostly divided between school, church, and the soccer field as a means of escaping stress. Now that I think about it, I am almost thirty years old, and for over twenty of those years, I have been constantly stressed in every aspect of my life. This stress took a toll on my physical health, resulting in back problems, illness, and poor eating habits due to financial constraints. I survived on cheap food from discount stores, like ramen and hot Cheetos, until I developed stomach ulcers. Mentally and emotionally, I felt like I was crumbling and on the verge of giving up due to the stress and anxiety of not having a stable home for most of my life.

Furthermore, in my younger years, I understood the importance of keeping quiet and staying focused on my education to avoid any trouble. I was able to achieve some remarkable accomplishments, such as winning awards in sports and being recognized for my inspiration. However, amidst these achievements, I realized that there was something more significant at stake: my soul. Now, as I approach thirty, I reflect on whether I have truly been living or simply surviving, even as a self-proclaimed Christian. Despite my knowledge of scripture, I question if I have truly spent quality time with God, who has declared my worth and potential. Why do I continue to see myself as less than, when the truth is right in front of me? I must open the book and immerse myself in its teachings, not out of obligation, but with the understanding that my life depends on it. For as it is written, 'Man shall not live on bread alone, but by every Word of God.

So, I inquired about the nourishment I was allowing myself to consume, both in terms of food and words. What kind of words was I absorbing and internalizing? Were they words of negativity and self-doubt, or words of truth, wisdom, and empowerment? For instance, did I listen more to the words that said I wasn't intelligent enough, leading me to give up on education, or to the words that belittled me instead of acknowledging my worth? The truth is that I am capable of achieving anything with strength from a higher power, and I am more than a conqueror. I am fearfully and wonderfully made, and it is not my place to seek revenge. All I need to do is keep moving forward, without dwelling on past mistakes.

Hence, if I have faith in Jesus, then all my transgressions are forgiven, and the debt has been fully paid. It makes me wonder why I dwell on my past mistakes, sins, and behaviors when Jesus has already atoned for them once and for all. There is no reason to revisit them. By believing the lies instead of the truth, I allowed my adversary to remind me of my past shortcomings (not being good enough, always falling short, lacking intelligence or speed, and going nowhere), disregarding the still, calm, and gentle voice that speaks the truth. I acknowledge that I chose to listen to falsehoods instead of the truth because that is what I was accustomed to, but now is the time to decide and heed the truth of what the Scriptures say about me. Consequently, the more I continued in this manner of living, the less fruitful my life became. In essence, I was merely accepting the circumstances I was dealt with, rather than truly living. As a follower of Christ, I should be living confidently, as a victorious conqueror, taking ownership of my life and actively living out the teachings of the Word. Something needed to change. I had to mature and recognize that this is my life to live, and I have the choice to allow the chaos and evil of the world to consume me or to lift my head high, take responsibility for my life, and face it with confidence, knowing my true identity.

Chapter 4

The Wondering

It took approximately fifteen years for me to pause everything and eliminate certain aspects of my life to surrender to the will of God. This was the wake-up call I needed. I realized the importance of praying to God and engaging in meaningful communication while also practicing the art of listening. I find it intriguing how some people can engage in group discussions without truly listening, either talking incessantly or pretending to listen just to interject their thoughts. In contrast, I recognized the need to genuinely listen to God as I cried out for His guidance in living my life one step at a time. I was uncertain where to begin or how to start, especially since I had spent most of my life without a voice. However, as I started using my voice, I realized that it wasn't just about what I said, but also about how I said it. More importantly, it was about listening to God and allowing His Word to speak directly to me, guiding me on when to stay and when to move. I used to pray, 'In the name of Jesus!' hoping that the people around me would stop controlling me. I longed to be in heaven, free from pain. Have you ever reached a point where you wanted to give up, regardless of your faith, without realizing that God might be urging you to step back and simply have a heartfelt conversation with Him, just like His Son did? Throughout most of my fifteen years as a 'Christian,' I found myself complaining to God about all the meaningless noise in my life, without taking the time to listen to His voice in the midst of it all. Eventually, God began to confront me with His Word, showing me that it wasn't the control of others that affected me, but rather my lack of belief in who I truly am and to whom I belong. In cultivating a proactive relationship with God, rather than a reactive one, I began to understand that I needed to undergo pruning, cutting away, and personal transformation. I needed to embrace silence and be attentive to God's voice, rather than seeking attention through idle chatter. I needed to be slow to anger and quick to listen and comprehend, understanding that the voices I choose to listen to can shape my future.

Besides embarking on my spiritual journey with God, I recall feeling stuck at a pivotal moment. Although I believed I had heard His voice, I soon realized that I had twisted His teachings to suit my desires, straying from His divine plan. God was urging me to be proactive rather than reactive. My emotional attachment to my church roles and the people associated with it caused me to overreact, but I failed to recognize that God is a possessive deity. He desires my every thought, desire, action, and vision. Do you remember when I first started attending church at fifteen and sought validation from others rather than from God? That was an instance where God reminded me to examine myself before causing harm. As I distanced myself from my previous life and established this relationship with God, my faith began to flourish. I genuinely believed in His promises to make me His child, a member of His royal priesthood, a co-heir to His throne, and adopted into His kingdom. I not only embraced my calling but also faithfully accepted it. This calling entails living a life of freedom and peace amidst trials and tribulations, allowing God to restore my well-being through His teachings. I can now not only love God and His word but also remain devoted to the person Christ has called me to be. Remember when I questioned the meaning of the cross? It was right in front of me, and I had the choice to embrace it. The cross symbolizes a willingness to live for God unconditionally, sacrificing everything to gain His approval rather than the approval of humanity or myself.

I was suddenly overwhelmed by the idea of 'Do I truly know who I am now, as seen through the eyes of my spiritual self, and do I understand where I truly belong?' Doubt and indecision have no place in the Kingdom of God, yet growing up, I was accustomed to being uncertain of myself. This was a wake-up call from God as I began to have conversations with Him about life. I came to realize that both Heaven and Hell are unwavering and not conflicted. For instance, Satan's tactics of stealing, killing, and destroying have never changed. Similarly, God's Word remains steadfast in its promise of bringing abundant life. It is common for us as humans to speak both blessings and curses, whether we identify as Christians or not. Some individuals may praise you as an angel one day, but if you repeatedly do something they disapprove of, they may label you as a devil and turn away from you. However, if Heaven and Hell remain united and undivided, why are people who claim to be followers of Christ, like me, often plagued by doubt and division? Why is there discord within the church? If we are truly focused on the Father's work, shouldn't we move forward together for the Kingdom of God, despite our disagreements, and refrain from dwelling on past hurts and regrets? In the Bible, the disciples did not always see eye to eye (especially Paul and Peter, who had strong faith), but they died as early martyrs for the Kingdom of Heaven because their faith remained unwavering. Why are so many religious marriages failing among families who attend or do not attend church? Why are children growing up without proper guidance from leaders in various aspects of their lives, whether it be church leaders, teachers, coaches, peers, or especially their parents?

Inquire these inquiries so that I can directly approach the divine word and converse with our Heavenly Father, Spirit, and His Son

(Jesus) concerning now. Now is the opportune moment to genuinely sit down and grapple with the Divine. His word inquires, 'how is it that when the Spirit of Truth descends upon you, or when you request, you shall receive if you are not uncertain or vacillating?' Remember, he spoke of faith as a mustard seed. You may declare that the mountain will relocate over there, and it shall indeed move; in other words, have an unwavering belief in your heart that you trust in what God promises to accomplish. However, you must fulfill your role. Have faith and be guided by the Divine Spirit. After a period of separation from my previous associations and activities, the voices quieted down and His teachings enlightened my mind. As a result, I transformed. Instead of harboring bitterness towards others, I chose to embrace a more positive way of life. This involved actively seeking peace, showing mercy, and maintaining faith in God's unwavering support. By identifying myself as His child, the joy within my being - encompassing my body, mind, soul, and spirit - remains unassailable.

In an instant, I found myself in the most exposed and defenseless state of mind and being that I had ever experienced. Exposed and defenseless, just like Adam and Eve in the Garden. God called out to them, and they responded, 'Here we are, Lord.' Well, here I was in this phase of life, saying to Him, 'Here I am.' Here is the complete and unfiltered version of Rebekah. The one who was a savior to everyone else while trying to escape from her own pain and chaotic life. Hitting rock bottom, with no one to lift me, it was our Father who brushed off the dust and carried me on His shoulders. He not only nursed me back to health, but also held me accountable. The scriptures say that the Lord disciplines those He loves, so we should not be discouraged when correction comes from our Father's love. And oh, how much correction I needed in my life. There I was, on my knees with my arms outstretched. Not because I was giving up on life, but because I knew I couldn't move forward without God carrying me through it all. I rediscovered the power of the Spirit to lead, guide, and directme into all truths. Then came the shedding of the old layers, like a snake shedding its skin.

To grow and develop, one must first let go of everything they thought they knew. This was true for me when I decided to strip away my preconceived notions. Some may question why I left the church, but I believe that true wisdom comes from personal understanding, not blind instruction. The fruit of my life was lacking depth and meaning, despite the good deeds I was doing within the church community. I realized that simply going through the motions wasn't enough. I needed a genuine, private relationship with God. I now find myself seeking a personal connection with our Heavenly Father, and He has welcomed me with open arms into His family.

Institutional customs and conditions have taught us many lessons. One aspect that might change is how we perceive the true presence of the divine in the Church. What defines a church, you may ask? According to scripture, wherever two or more gather, the divine is there. So, is it possible to have a church-like experience while sitting in an El Pollo Loco and discussing spirituality? I think so. However, it is important to acknowledge that many devout churchgoers may contest this notion, arguing that one must be connected to a physical church building. While there is nothing inherently wrong with this perspective, I pose a question: what kind of spiritual fruits are being produced in your life? The quality of a tree can be discerned by the fruits it bears. I also question the idea of being exclusively connected to any one institution. If one is firmly attached to a church, it becomes exceedingly difficult to detach oneself from it. There is often a great deal of judgment and disdain directed towards individuals who choose to leave the church. In my personal experience, God challenged me to examine the state of my spiritual growth, leading me to make significant changes. This involved shedding the titles and positions of leadership within the church to establish a genuine relationship with God.

Furthermore, I understand that leaving a church can be difficult for those involved, but one might question if God was calling them elsewhere. However, it is important to consider if their hearts were truly aligned with God. Personally, when I left the church, I realized that my intentions were misguided. I believed I was seeking a deeper connection with God in a smaller congregation, but in reality, I had been running away from God my entire life, whether I was attending church or not. If I were in church, I would avoid cultivating a personal relationship with God by focusing on leadership roles and being overly involved. On the other hand, if I wasn't attending church, I would distract myself with sports or spending time with friends to escape the truth that my life was in disarray and need of significant transformation both externally and internally. In essence, we have been conditioned to prioritize our outward appearance while neglecting the inner filth that may exist. To put it simply, pigs don't recognize their stench. In other words, churchgoers have become accustomed to conforming to certain behaviors and attitudes, which may have caused many of us to lose sight of having a genuine, authentic relationship with God. I acknowledge that I stayed away because I was afraid to confront my life following God's will. Instead, I clung to my desires, barely surviving rather than thriving in life.

I was simply satisfied with listening to sermons from other pastors and preachers, taking away their teachings without seeking the word for myself. I felt uplifted by what I heard, but I failed to realize that God was urging me to wake up and move forward toward the blessings that awaited me. It made me reflect on the Israelites, who spent forty years wandering in the desert after being freed from slavery, constantly complaining along the way. Similarly, I had professed my faith in Jesus as my Lord and Savior, but I didn't know how to cultivate a personal relationship with

God while engaging in religious activities like attending church, leading ministries, and participating in various groups. This left me in a desert of uncertainty. I found myself questioning who I was and where I was headed, feeling lost and deeply confused.

By ceasing all activities both within and outside of the church, I found myself uncertain of my direction. However, God began to reveal to me through various means that I was about to embark on a magnificent journey alongside Him. It all began amid my wilderness.

Chapter 5

Where am I?

This is a chapter about my journey with God throughout my life. It's not just about where I was during challenging times, but also about how God and I reconciled. Let's start with the times when my car broke down and I had financial struggles. Despite the difficulties, God was with me. I felt lost and alone, but God never abandoned me. I wasn't taught important life skills, but God's word showed me the right way to live. He helped me overcome afflictions and navigate the harsh realities of the world.

During a difficult time in my life, my car broke down in a dangerous area while I was on my way to my second job. I felt overwhelmed and desperate for a way out. Although I questioned why I was facing so many challenges, I remembered that God promised to guide us through adversity. As I worked two full-time jobs and slept in parking lots, I relied on unconventional sources of sustenance like fast food and makeshift accommodations. It became clear that I couldn't rely on my strength to get me out of this situation, but I trusted that God was working something positive amidst it all.

In what way was any of this beneficial? I am just beginning my relationship with God. I have taken on financial obligations and now I am struggling to keep my head above water. I am only scratching the surface of what it means to live out my faith in God. However, I am also realizing that I am in significant financial debt. I have learned to be humble before experiencing honor and to listen to God's calming voice saying, 'Do not be afraid, I am your God. I am not only leading the way, but I am also with you in this moment.' All I needed to do was trust in Him to guide me towards truth and righteousness. By placing my faith in Him and understanding my identity, I no longer felt lost and confused. I knew that it was not my strength that allowed me to stand firm, but the power of God within me. It was not about where I was during this time, but about where He was. He remained by my side, went ahead of me, and continues to pave the way as I write these words guided by His influence.

Let's take it a step further into the emotions of it all. Life as I may have once known seemed to be snuffing out all the air and energy that I was trying to breathe in. There just didn't seem to be a way out. Though life around me seemed to get crazy with everyone's chatter. As the economy was inflating, God was teaching me to stand still as that was all I had left in me. For instance, gas prices were almost six dollars, and I had to fill up a one-hundred-and-thirty-dollar tank on minimum wage. Feeling as if the air was getting sucked out right under me as my guardian chose to look away and not give a helping hand when faced with hardship. My guardian would just laugh at me and say, 'Now how do you like it?' As if I had become a nobody to this individual and I would not make it through this life. My guardian would pounce and harp on me whenever I seemed to not understand anything and practically call me out as being stupid or dumb with her choices of words. I found it harder than choosing the voices I was listening to. The voices of the liar saying I wasn't good enough or listening to the truth that I may have not understood, but I can always ask the right questions to the right people to gain knowledge and not feel like a failure anymore. When the Bible says that our tongue has the power to bring life or death to one another, that is real talk and one hundred percent accurate. I felt as if my life was being snuffed out by the words that came from the Liar that almost stole all my joy inside of me, almost killed my chances at ever loving myself, and almost destroyed my spirit from ever truly living in freedom and peace. Yet, because I chose to live this life, I started training myself to listen to the truth of what the living word of God says. That this Word became life and life was through a human that was fully man and God all at the same time and made His dwelling among us. I remember studying this word for so long, yet couldn't quite catch that relationship part, but now that I am meditating on it day and night and talking with God a little bit more each day, I am beginning to walk away and not listen to the lives of others around me who are chained up and bound by the Father of lies. In addition, I chose not to listen to the lies of the world and what it may have deemed me to be, yet I listened to every word of God and what He has said. Again, man shall not live by bread alone, but by every word of God.

I once heard that the only difference between a poor and wealthy individual is their mindset. While I struggled to reconstruct my life and strive towards purchasing a home, I discovered myself offering people transportation to church without receiving any money for gas and encountering resentment within my household. I even spent a weekend sleeping in my car simply to find some tranquility and seclusion. Despite feeling like I was consistently lagging, I had to reassess my beliefs and objectives. I reminded myself that I was fortunate to not be living on the streets or entangled in perilous circumstances. However, I knew I needed to aim higher and think differently to progress and avoid remaining stagnant in life. Living in a shared space for a decade has given me financial stability. Money and wisdom can solve problems, as our God promises to prosper and give hope.

Knowing my identity and purpose shapes my future. I focus on the path ahead, not dwelling on the past. Trusting in God, who is rebuilding my foundation, is key. I move forward without hesitation. Just as you as the reader may think or assume that all the above was about over, let me continue to elaborate on how my feelings and emotions were at war with my conscience and mentality trying to move forward into God's calling on my life.

In what state of mind was I when it appeared that others were attacking me psychologically, mentally, emotionally, and verbally, yet I chose to remain silent? It appeared as though everything was fine on the surface, but internally I felt my spirit being torn apart. Going to work gave me a sense of belonging more than being with those I lived with. Attending church felt hollow as others expected me to constantly give of myself. I couldn't pinpoint my exact location, but I did realize that I was reaching a breaking point. I was on the verge of losing control, and it wouldn't be a pleasant sight. So, where was I again? Let me think... I was right in the midst of where God intended me to be.

This may have been a puzzle to me but not to him. He was taking action on my behalf when I couldn't even take one step. Little did I know that the Divine was rearranging the course of my life. The Divine was shaping me into the likeness of what He called me to be in His divine plan and not how I should be in society by my desires. The realm of designations and tags. Can we refer to this as the battle for my essence and consciousness? My physical self was inclined to fight and cling to this body of mine and just be satisfied with mere survival, while my spiritual self-kept propelling me forward to thrive mentally, physically, and spiritually. The Spirit of the Divine was communicating with my thoughts and emotions, saying, 'It's time for transformation.' If you find this chapter peculiar at any point, then you are correct because it was peculiar for me as well. It was peculiar for me to pause my life and activities to truly perceive what the Divine saw in me, let alone believe in it. The part where I am 'chosen' and 'called out by name' is when I feel like I am hitting rock bottom again with debts and no place to live except my car. The Divine's teachings say, 'Don't just listen to the teachings, but put them into practice.' I needed to take action and keep pushing forward, not just to have a personal connection with the Divine, but to live a life of abundance in the blessings that were waiting for my family and me.

My life as a believer in Christ, I believed that I was fulfilling my calling by serving as a leader in the ministry for the homeless, the youth, and those in recovery within the church community for over ten years. However, upon reflection, I came to a realization. My conscience spoke to my inner being, warning me that I was in a precarious situation. If I didn't fully embrace the teachings of Christ and trust in God's guidance as I navigate through life, I could potentially become what society had already labeled me as even before my birth. This could mean imprisonment, falling victim to human trafficking, or ending up impoverished and addicted to drugs. The generational curse that has plagued my family could persist, and if I fail to address my issues, I might pass these burdens onto the next generation. I would become even worse off than my biological mother, as my guardian would conclude.

However, divine intervention occurred when God rebuked these voices, commanding them to retreat. The authority of God's words instills fear in the enemy and revives life within the lifeless. With only one life to live, I pondered how to make the most of it. As mentioned earlier, the tongue possesses the power to speak life or death. According to the Bible, I possess what I declare, so what shall I choose to declare today? Furthermore, as I journey through life, I must remember that in the end, it is only the Creator who will judge me. This realization became a turning point for me.

Recognizing that God is my ultimate judge, I resolved to commune with Him daily, not merely daily, but even on an hourly or minute-by-minute basis. Since God is my judge, I can approach Him before anyone else. I came to understand that I had unconsciously taken on the burdens of others while neglecting my own (that is, my own life). Conversely, I had been wasting God's precious time by disregarding the calling of my own life and focusing solely on helping others, living in their shadows. Despite being there for everyone, I still felt inadequate, running around aimlessly and feeling isolated, while drowning in every aspect of my being. I was drained financially, mentally, emotionally, psychologically, physically, and above all, spiritually. Despite my flaws and successes, God was always with me. Now, I'm learning to have unwavering faith as I follow God's calling for my life. With God, all things are possible. In this narrative about my chosen lifestyle, I have come to embrace the belief that through Christ, who empowers me, I can accomplish anything. I am gradually aligning myself with God's strength and reducing my own. Here are a few insights and knowledge I have gained on my journey.

Chapter 6

Whom I belong to?

Before commencing this chapter, I want to emphasize that I was both alarmed and disheartened when I embarked on this connection with God. Having lived my entire life without any strong and stable relationships, including one with God, I finally decided to surrender myself and initiate a personal relationship with Him. Initially, this relationship was daunting as I allowed myself to be vulnerable and exposed to both criticism and abundant love. However, I repeatedly found myself frustrated by the corrections I received while starting this relationship. I was accustomed to pretending and faking my way through life, rather than truly understanding my identity, purpose, and future. I came to realize that I had been in denial of my true potential and had been fixated on my past lies and failures, which the Father of lies wanted me to focus on. I no longer needed to harbor anger or bitterness toward those who saw me as insignificant. Instead, I could now choose to live out the rest of my days in a blossoming and eternal relationship with our Father, who guides us toward truth and righteousness.

In the realm of spirituality, it is not only important to know oneself and find a sense of belonging, but also to understand who one belongs to. Despite feeling like a constant disappointment to my guardians, I felt a calling from God to let go of my ways and surrender my life to Him. This meant relinquishing my knowledge, dreams, desires, and expectations, and putting my complete trust in God. As I released my careless way of living, I began to recognize where my help truly came from. Although my ego resisted, I realized the need to confront my arrogance and immaturity to grow. Through studying God's Word and seeking His counsel, my relationship with Him grew stronger. I learned that true strength lies in humbling oneself and accepting correction, even if it may appear weak to others. This process of correction allowed me to gain knowledge and understanding, like the pruning of a tree, and see things more clearly.

I realized that I was taking dangerous paths and decided to remove them from my life to stay connected with my relationship with God. Instead of just going to church and getting caught up in serving in various roles, I chose to let go of my titles and positions within the church so that I could truly focus on my relationship with God. I was tired of going through the motions and feeling spiritually empty. I longed for a genuine relationship and a fresh start. I didn't want to settle for just going to another church organization without knowing what to do with my life. I let go of everything I had done and knew, and I noticed that the results of my efforts were either short-lived or unsatisfying. I realized that I had been trying to live my life on my own, pretending to have it all together, without relying on God or others around me. Before opening myself up to a relationship with God, I could see that I was slowly losing myself, despite the illusion of being fine because I went to church and did good deeds. But now, in a true relationship with God, my spirit is clinging to the presence of God's Spirit within me, and my soul is no longer thirsty.

According to popular belief, doing the same thing repeatedly and expecting different results is considered 'insanity'. In my case, I was caught in a cycle of attending church, taking on numerous ministries, and exhausting myself to the point where my relationship with God suffered. To start anew, I had to acknowledge that God wouldn't chastise me forever. If I didn't make a change and turn away from my mistakes, He would eventually turn His back on me. I needed to humble myself, trust in God completely, and embrace the life He had called me to live. Through repentance and seeking forgiveness, I found a fresh start. As I reconciled my relationship with God, I let go of bitterness and anger towards those who displayed arrogance, realizing that I too had been arrogant. By softening my heart, I opened myself up to the guidance and direction of the Holy Spirit in my life.

In the Scriptures, Paul speaks of the constant struggle he faced. I too experienced a similar struggle, with my desires conflicting with the divine Spirit within me. The Spirit of God, that is. I tended to resist submission and control, but little did I know that surrendering everything to God was the ultimate path. God is aware of all my thoughts and actions, and He desires for me to offer them as a sacrifice. The Scriptures teach us to present our bodies as a living sacrifice, holy and pleasing to Him. This is the true and proper way to worship. As I shifted my focus from pleasing others to pleasing the Lord, my mind underwent a process of renewal. Pleasing people is vastly different from pleasing God. While the Lord invites us to come as we are, people often take without giving in return, especially when it comes to our time. Time is considered a valuable asset, and wasting it is irreversible. To allow God to work in my life, I needed to surrender everything and follow Him wholeheartedly. This act of submission pleases Him. Pleasing God also involves having childlike faith, which I struggled with since I used to rely on myself during my upbringing and the challenges of daily life.

Starting anew with the one who raised me, I faced rejection and animosity. I worked my way up to a safer car, becoming smarter and wiser in taking care of myself. I had to learn how to build credit and start my adult life from scratch. Despite the weight of oppression and depression, God was with me. I had to change my habits with God's help. Instead of letting life happen to me, I chose to live and move forward. It was challenging, but God was doing a good job in me, and I trusted the process. I was afraid to embrace my potential and have a relationship with God. Growing up, I learned not to trust and assumed the worst about myself. I was scared of being judged and predicted to fail. These habits were influenced by my upbringing and society. But now, I realize that I just need to listen to God's voice in my life.

I was very content with the familiarity and the customs of not only this world but also the traditions and conditions within the church. I assumed that I should attend church and be involved in its daily activities while adhering to its traditions. I played the role of a churchgoer without truly believing or fully committing myself to developing a deep relationship with God. However, when I started to personally engage with the teachings and make them a part of my life, the word of God became alive to me. Previously, there was no passion or enthusiasm for the word in my life, but now it began to have a profound impact. In other words, the word of God became tangible and its power started to take full effect. God revealed himself to be more real in my life and I discovered a true, unwavering relationship with Him. He became the family I had longed for and I realized that I could openly communicate and walk with Him. I could share my deepest secrets without fear of ridicule, for He is a loving Father who took the time to guide me and help me understand the consequences of my actions as I moved forward. I can always hear His voice inside of me, saying what a good God He is. He is the Good God for whom He says, "I am". I'm that loving Father in times of storm and will protect you. He has fought many battles and many wars and mine was just one more victory for him (To God be all glory and praise). That was and is how much I meant and still mean to Him. It wasn't just one more victory for Him, but it was personal. It made me feel like I was the only one He cared for at that moment in time. Again, thanks be to God our Father, I needed that sounding love!

Knowing that I can truly lean on Him as he keeps my arms held high to never fall nor fail. Not only was I stepping on Holy ground but the Holy ground that I stepped upon belonged to me too; hence why, it was personal. In this, God made me cry many tears of my sorrows, but He also had me smile many tears of my release that I can trust in Him fully. Not just a one-minute Father but an every day Father for the rest of my life that was not going to leave nor forsake me eternally. This was the part where I began to surrender more of myself; in return, I would begin to love more of Him in time. I can say that this was my father's and I's dance in life. This was the Father who loved me more than the father who was never present when I was growing up. He is the Father who leads and guides me. He put His word on His word and moved me into my destiny. Not only did He preach what He preached, but He preached what He practiced.

This is the Divine Being who parted the Red Sea. It was He who liberated the prisoners and that includes me. You are aware of that section where He stated, 'I will remain by your side closer than a brother?' Well, He meant much more to me. He assured me that no harm would come my way because He had truly set me free. As I paused and reflected, I chose to have faith. If there was a towering peak, He promised to be there. If there was a deep valley, He assured me He'd be there too. If there was a battle, He declared me the conqueror even before it commenced. He assured me that He would never abandon or forsake me. He stated that even if heaven and earth were to vanish, His words would never fail. He assured me of His support, but in return, He asked, 'Did you hear me?' I was there for you when you called out and wept to me. I was there for you when no one wanted you to hear from me and when the world tried to make you turn away from me. It was I who kept beckoning you to come to me.

In the realm of spirituality, the righteous often face numerous challenges. However, I have rescued you from all of them and will leave no stone unturned. I offer you a sanctuary of tranquility and harmony, a gift that I bestow upon you. All I ask is for you to keep your faith in me, as I have always been by your side. This is a profound love story that is overflowing with emotions. The divine connection between my God and the unfamiliar deity becomes familiar to me. Our heavenly father, who resides in the celestial realm, deserves our utmost reverence. He takes center stage in my life, with no room for backstage passes. Holy Spirit, I implore you, will you walk beside me and guide me in dancing with my heavenly Father's divine essence? I rely on your guidance to lead me in the right direction. I discovered that my Heavenly Father desires so much more for me that it moved me to tears. He is not only a father, but the best Father one could ever hope for. The Father I have yearned for all these years. With my spirit, I beseech you, show me your ways, Lord, and guide me along the path of righteousness. I can hear my spirit pleading with my physical self, show me your ways, Lord. At this moment, my physical self submits to the Spirit, as it elevates me to a life of righteousness in His presence. His Spirit declares that there shall be no more of the old ways, and I shall rise and fulfill the purpose He has called me to. The true essence of God's love transcends the shallow understanding that the world attempts to imprint on my heart. God proclaimed that although I was broken, I shall rise and live as His ambassador. As His child, I choose to live because He has spoken, "I say to you, live." This is no longer how it used to be. Previously, I spent six days a week assisting others, neglecting to care for myself. For instance, I would offer rides to and from church without expecting any compensation for the fuel expenses. Yet,

God always made a way to ensure that people continued to come and hear His word. I dedicated my time to the youth, from their early years in elementary school to their final year of high school. I participated in their events and became an integral part of their lives. However, in doing all these things, I failed to invest in my future. I consider these acts as small miracles, although they felt like mountains at the time. Nevertheless, God never abandoned me during this period. I can confidently say that not only is God good, but He is also faithful and just. As the scripture says, be faithful in the little things, and He will bless you abundantly. My spirit began to stir and come alive.

So here I stood with a car as my literal dwelling, back to a low-paying full-time job, burdened with significant debt, and with God drawing me nearer than ever before and delivering powerful wake-up calls in my life so that I could begin to live my life with God in liberation and abundance. When I believed that I had never been taught anything in life, I simply hadn't been seeking guidance from the right source and asking the right questions to live my life. God had been present all along, and now I can embark on a new chapter in my life and choose to live each day, rather than merely surviving. The voices of falsehoods and the oppressor began to fade away as the voice of God, the Father of all truths, resounded loudly and clearly.

It was a profound moment for my spirit when Jesus spoke the words, 'Let he who is without fault cast the first stone.' In that instant, I realized that my guardian had her share of imperfections. She tried to pass on her generational curse to me, based on the pain that had plagued her. However, the power of God's Word prevented that curse from taking hold of me and my future. The Word of God declares that those whom He sets free are truly free. Therefore, I was encouraged to go forth and sin no more. Unfortunately, my guardian ended up perpetuating the cycle of hurt and oppression that was passed down to her from her parents.

And I, being the next generation, became the recipient of this curse. I never realized that my guardian raised me to serve her, constantly reminding me that I owed her my life and blaming me for her miseries. She refused to release me from the chains of her mistakes, even as she listened to influential preachers. The more they preached, the more she burdened me. The more I tried to please her, the more she crushed me further into the dust. She attempted to teach me from her errors or accused me of committing mistakes that were never mine. She repeatedly declared that I would never amount to anything. It was then that I understood how her upbringing, ridicule, and belittlement had shaped me. I felt like a sacrificial lamb when her two husbands passed away, as she kept a close watch on my every move and controlled my finances as an example.

She was burdened and haunted by her past, unsure of her ultimate fate. Despite her despair, she offered me no hope. In times like these, when guidance from parents fails, I am grateful for the wisdom of the elderly who once said, 'someone was praying for me.' It is a testament to the power of prayer that even if it wasn't my guardian, there were individuals who interceded for me in different seasons of my life. For that, I am truly thankful for those people.

My guardian faced many challenges in her upbringing, including strained relationships with her sister and mother, as well as accusing her father of infidelity. Although she found solace in the church, it's unclear if the teachings truly resonated with her. Despite claiming to never lie, I discovered that this was untrue. Coming home from work, I would often be criticized for even the smallest mistakes, like not cleaning the bathroom drain. Living with a parent who didn't get what she wanted made me feel like I couldn't attain what I wanted in life either. Despite loving my guardian, my love was never sufficient for her. She would demean and degrade me, claiming that I owed her my life. If I had chosen to live solely for her, I wouldn't have a life of my own. Growing up, my only goal was to survive in an environment devoid of hope.

However, that serene and tranquil voice was enticing me back to His unwavering and redeeming affection that He had for me. It was intimate. How could it be when the Divine Essence arises within you? Thank you, Jesus. Not only has he assured me that I am the path, the veracity, the vitality, but he challenged me to uncover 'who I am' in Him. That it wasn't all the voices of the underlings echoing in my mother's soul, but I am the offspring of the living God. The one who came and sacrificed on the cross to restore me completely. The Supreme Being who affirmed my goodness while perfecting me. The multitude of these voices were losing their hold on me while the Divine Essence entered to fill me to the brim with His presence. As the Sacred Scriptures began to flourish in my Inner Being, I began to flourish. The shackles of attachment that my guardian had on me are now shattered. No longer was I proclaiming that I was a failure as my guardian declared. No longer spoke death to myself, but I chose to live with Christ who had illuminated His presence upon my existence. How could it be when the Divine Essence arises within you to love your neighbor as yourself? To love someone who could never love themselves. God was about to steer my life on a different path.

According to the saying, a dog consumes its vomit. Similarly, when people grow tired or bored of something they've created, they often return to what feels familiar or comfortable. For instance, I desire to become a billionaire, but I lack the motivation to put in the necessary effort, thus remaining financially broke. To experience growth and success, one must step out of their comfort zone and embrace the unknown. We are all temporary beings, as it has been written that we shall return to dust. Now, let's address the question: what do I believe based on my faith? Did I believe I was insignificant? Perhaps in the past, during my upbringing, but not anymore. I believe that in this life, we will face trials and tribulations. However, I also have faith that God will deliver the righteous from their afflictions, including myself. Now, what about the concern of getting bored? For most of my life, I constantly felt restless and bored, always searching for something new. Yet, I eventually realized that I wasn't truly in control. When it comes to the calling God has placed on my life, will I grow weary or will I remain steadfast in His word, without doubt or indecision? Faith requires us to do what others are not doing.

At almost thirty, sitting in a McDonald's parking lot, I was questioned about my connection with God. If you truly love God, you should also love yourself since you were made in His image. So, if you truly love yourself, why don't you care about what happens to you? For example, instead of finding a safe place to sleep when running out of gas, you choose to sleep in the woods where there's danger. And when it comes to improving your financial situation, you hesitate to explore other opportunities. You blame others for things you could have done yourself, like blaming your family for not raising you properly. Are you content with living paycheck to paycheck like this for the rest of your life? Do you truly have a connection with God? If yes, where is the evidence of it? Reflecting on my own experience, I realized that the fruit of my faith was mostly seen in church activities rather than in my relationship with God. I was focused on pleasing others and not on cultivating a genuine connection with God. This realization made me question if I ever truly had a relationship with God.

I was living my life in the name of Christ, but I hadn't fully allowed Him to enter every aspect of my life. I felt like a failure and wanted to give up. It reminded me of when I had to quit playing soccer due to financial constraints. But this was different - it was a matter of life and death. I had to choose between quitting or surrendering everything to follow God. I had to make daily sacrifices, be loyal to God's word, and stay grounded in His will. It wasn't easy, but I had to go beyond what others thought of me and pursue a deeper relationship with Him. Choosing this life completely transformed my world. I had to let go of everything I knew for God to reveal His higher thoughts and ways to me. To grow and mature, I had to go through a process of deconstruction and stripping away. This required me to be quiet, and humble, ask the right questions, and not be careless about life. Let me take you back to the beginning and uncover the origins.

Chapter 7

From the Voices came the Silence

My children know my voice and strangers won't follow. Did I truly know the voice of God? The word does say that wherever the Spirit of the Lord is, there is freedom. Where was my freedom, and did I even know what that freedom looked or felt like? When the word says to train up a child in how they should grow up, the child sees and hears who teaches them to live. For most of my personal life I was not raised and grew up on how to get or search for this relationship with God. The word also says to search for Him like hidden treasure. Growing up, I was searching for so many other things and none of them were getting to know God in a personal relationship. So, if there was freedom then why had I been swarmed by feelings of shame and past regret, loneliness, and always missing the mark and being that failure yet again behind closed doors? I knew at church I "felt" good because I was good with everyone; however, when I got home there was so much strife and animosity with the one whom I had been living with all my life. Never brought up or tried to resolve the hidden and dark secrets. The hidden curses on our family lineage, the darkness of being oppressed and suppressed within poverty, and curses that come out of our mouths and not blessings. Being born into and surrounded by constant regrets, the pain of being hurt, the ongoing anger, and the generational curses that were being passed down. No wonder I wanted to die when I was growing up.

Nearly approaching thirty, stepping away from church affiliations, and ministries, and living away from my guardian, it dawned on me that I was about to approach this new relationship with our Father. I would soon call this a newfound relationship. In the Word, it says come to me all who are weary, and I will give you rest. He said that his rod and staff would comfort me in the days of my trouble, and He would deliver me from all afflictions. In searching for this relationship, I heard Him calling me away from others and into Him. Away from the noise and chatter that was in this world whether it be in a church setting, a home setting, or in a ministry setting. He was calling me out of organizations to draw me into a personal relationship with Him. It was Him that awakened my soul and quickened my spirit. In other words, He shook up my spirit man inside of me to draw me closer to Him. To offer me another go around in life and live a life of freedom and no longer a life of oppression or depression. He was calling me out into the unknown where I would embark on this adventure with Him. To take this grand leap of faith, I not only needed to be a hearer of the word but a doer of the word as well.

In the realm of conflicting emotions, contemplation, and curiosity, 'why?'. Although I had numerous questions, I never experienced anxiety because I was aware that He was by my side and would never abandon me. I questioned why He had called upon me now, to which He simply replied, 'You came to me when you were ready, and now you are prepared.' Knowing that He was with me every step of the way, He addressed the queries I had during that season. However, it was my soul that yearned for healing and restoration for me to truly live. I recall asking who would fill the void within my spirit. I expressed my uneasiness and frustration in embarking on a relationship with God. It required immense faith to surrender myself to God and mend what was broken, including my pride. Deep down, I recognized that my soul was burdened by generational curses, which left me feeling hopeless. However, through my connection with our Father, I understood that He would never abandon me. This serves as a small example of my decision to listen and communicate with the comforting and serene voice of God, disregarding the lies of the enemy and even my internal voices.

How could I have felt as if I had already succumbed, but someone started to revive my body? Well, allowing His Divine Energy to lead, guide, and direct me into all truth and righteousness is a good starting point. Was I practicing what I preached and was heading in the direction that God called me in, or had I been succumbing to the ancestral burdens that were trying to take hold of me all along? Knowing now that God was, is, and will continue to be with me from here on out, I can commune with Him about these questions. I heard Him keep saying to me, don't be swayed by distractions, nor dwell on the past, but keep your focus on what lies ahead of you. To persevere in this journey and fulfill what God has called me to. This was necessary to emulate Jesus and offer the hope he had for everyone. Yes, life was not equitable, and yes, I have made many mistakes in this life; however, the Scriptures say this, 'That he who initiated a virtuous transformation in you will bring it to completion.' God is utilizing me to be His conduit to share the uplifting message about our identity to Him, and who He has been, is, and will continue to be for us.

Our divine parent becomes intimately involved when we communicate with them, not only in a formal group setting but also in our personal lives. They are always present, never abandoning us. We are all interconnected through their divine essence. Therefore, if we share the same divine parent, none of us have ever been forsaken. They have given us the gift of life on this earthly plane. Jesus remains the originator of our faith beyond this mortal existence.

In exploring how to live without fear of the future, I discovered the necessity of maintaining an ongoing connection with the Divine, whether it involved seeking clarity on biblical matters or grappling with life's complexities. This bond was unlike any other I had experienced in my earthly relationships - it was characterized by openness and authenticity. God tends to use imperfect individuals to advance His kingdom. Through this connection, I confronted the reality of my life's direction. I received constructive feedback when I strayed off course and found comfort in times of great hardship. This relationship with God was worth living for, worth dying for, and worth fighting for. It was an intimate connection that left no room for uncertainty - it was genuine and enduring, not a fleeting facade. I was beginning to develop a bond with the One who was restoring my broken existence and rebuilding my life from scratch. Our Father was the architect of a life that once felt empty of purpose, and He continued to create a magnificent masterpiece. This relationship taught me the significance of seeking wisdom, understanding, knowledge, and insight. It taught me to be a patient listener and to carefully choose my words.

In the Bible, it is said that the sheep know their shepherd's voice and won't follow a stranger. Similarly, I used to struggle to hear God's voice because I was too focused on pleasing others. But now, I have learned to tune out the noise of other people and listen to God's word. Even though I may have heard negative voices from my past, I now prioritize God's voice above all else.

I used to incline my ears to those around me and become their savior by helping them. In return, I never got the real help I needed while growing up due to looking as if I had it all together. I had been other people's answers to prayers yet failed at letting them go in pursuit of their relationship with the Father as they would keep coming back and putting their hope in me. Inevitably, I realized that I was doing the same thing in my personal life as well. I had become so comfortable being around others by helping them out and doing everything nearly exhausting myself while not facing the truth of getting to know the Father personally. Where it would be just Him and I. While continuing to pursue God in a personal relationship, nothing could compare to His great wisdom, understanding, grace, and truth. I was no longer listening to the past's names, ridicules, judgments, and lies, but I would listen to the living word of God. No longer was I a stranger to our Father's voice, but I now can tell His voice apart from all the others, especially the voices and lies from my past. My name was no longer a failure but more than a conqueror. No longer did I just sit around letting life happen before me and deem myself weak, but I took hold of His strength within my life to rise out of my own grave and choose to do something. I chose to believe that, no longer did the spirits of self-doubt, self-pity, depression, or anxiety consume me, but every word of God that breathed life back into my bones, reawakened me into the truth.

The truth means that wherever the Spirit of the Lord is there is freedom. This was my free ticket to live, and I took hold of it so that I could begin to live a life of peace and freedom. Sounds great and all, but to move forward with this ticket of freedom, our Father brought me back to a time in history when everything stopped, and it would become silent for three days. Three days of confusion and being scared to not lose their lives following Jesus Christ. Those people, meaning His disciples. Three days of pure sorrow out of a mother who gave birth to the Son of God and watched Him die a sinner's death on the cross as an innocent man. God told me that this life of peace and freedom was bought with a price, and I had to choose what I would do with it. This price was that our Father sent His Son to die for all of us. Our Father allowed His one and only Son to sacrifice Himself for us and die so that we could live with and for Him.

The Father led me to this crucifixion site where His son Jesus sacrificed himself for me. Through the nails that pierced His hands and feet, the spear that penetrated His side, the thorns that pierced His head, and His innocent blood that was shed not only for me but for all of humanity, for you and me. As I observed the wounds inflicted on His body from the inhumane whipping, these lashes tore His flesh apart with sharp stones attached to the whips. Despite His helplessness, He found the strength to carry the heavy cross on which He would eventually die. Before His flogging, He endured physical abuse, spitting, and mockery throughout His trial. This was God's Son, Jesus, betrayed by a disciple who kissed Him for thirty pieces of silver. Just moments after His arrest, all His disciples abandoned Him into the hands of the Roman guards. Furthermore, during His trial, one of His disciples, who later became a prominent figure in the church, denied knowing Jesus of Nazareth, and then the rooster crowed for the third time.

Our Heavenly Father led me to witness the crucifixion of His beloved Son, who was completely innocent, but it was the divine power of the Holy Spirit that brought Jesus back to life, triumphing over the forces of darkness. In this incredible act, Jesus not only defeated Satan but also liberated those who were held captive. Ultimately, it was through Jesus' sacrificial death and the resurrection power of the Holy Spirit that I received the gift of freedom. At the age of nearly thirty, God revealed to me that I too can rise above my struggles and live a life empowered by His strength, rather than relying on my own.

Chapter 8

Then came the ROAR

If I am going to die me, I might as well live me. And if I am going to live, I might as well be true to myself. I refuse to be held back by my past or the fears of the future. I will no longer let the hurt and pain inflicted by others control me. Instead, I choose to surrender my life to a higher power and serve as a representative. I will not be just another statistic or a useless tool. As I embark on this journey with my faith, a crucial question arises: Who am I, according to my beliefs? Jesus posed this question to me, urging me to examine my relationship with Him. Have I relied on others to define my connection to God, or have I sought a personal understanding? In the past, I placed my hope in God through others, which led them to place their trust in me instead of in our Father. Now, I intentionally seek the Lord's will in all things and strive to see Him in my everyday life. I no longer confine my spirituality to a checklist at church. Instead, I actively nurture my relationship with God throughout the week.

In my journey of faith, I have chosen to live wholeheartedly for God. Growing up, I realized the importance of having a family, but I discovered that true family is found in those who live out God's Word. Since I didn't have that kind of family in my personal life, I looked to our Heavenly Father to guide me. I also learned that even leaders in the church have their flaws and struggles. Many people come to church seeking hope and a relationship with God because they were never taught how to have one. If the pastors themselves are flawed, then who will teach them?

Express gratitude to Jesus for the Holy Spirit, our comforting guide who leads us to the truth. Embrace living by God's Word and dwelling in His presence. Seek Him and you will find Him, ask and it will be given. Through meditation on His Word, God has been teaching and guiding me. If you desire this relationship, simply talk to Him. Unfortunately, many in the church have been taught to view God as an authoritarian figure, discouraging questions and personal connection. Instead of nurturing relationships, they focused on memorization. This lack of personal connection led to gossip and a failure to understand grace and mercy. Perhaps they never received it. Consequently, they were bound by their past and hurt others. It's important to break this cycle by showing peace, mercy, and grace one step at a time.

Having a personal relationship with Christ brings freedom, hope, and light. It's not just about memorizing scriptures or being at the top, but about living out this relationship in our daily lives. Through the power of the Spirit, we find strength to face each day, repent, and experience a change of heart. Instead of relying on others, we actively seek God and His Word. Prioritizing self-care and seeking God's approval brings true fulfillment. When it comes to helping others, there is a fine line. We cannot force our help on those who do not want or are not ready for it. We have to respect people's free will. There is a saying, some will, some won't, so what next? In my opinion, I would choose to help the person in need who is asking for help, even if that person is me.

To fully surrender to God's plan every day and not my own. To empathize with those who are grieving and celebrate with those who are joyful, both inside and outside of the church. To mourn when hope seems lost, but still have unwavering faith in God's renewal of our strength. To rejoice in the wisdom and growth of others, and admire the courage and faith of martyrs around the world. The greatest love is to sacrifice for others, but it's important to also love and care for oneself. Without love, all our deeds are in vain. It's not enough to love our neighbors; we must love ourselves as well. Now is the time for me to follow God's will and live for His purpose, guided by the power of the Spirit.

In my mind, as I thought the questions were fading away, a new one emerged. If God is never too busy for me, why should I be too busy for Him? Other Christians are sacrificing everything for their faith, so why was it so difficult for me to open the Bible and read it? Wasn't I supposed to be an ambassador for Christ? If that's the case, then pleasing God should be my priority, not pleasing others. I can't help but wonder why there is so much division and noise in the church. Perhaps we have strayed from the true voice of God. The voice that speaks to our spirits, urging us to come home to our Father and live for His Kingdom's cause. Where is our faith? Where was mine? What good is it to gain the whole world if we don't have love? Love for ourselves, our neighbors, and our God. What good is a relationship that is shallow behind closed doors, hidden behind masks and titles? I used to rely on going to church to find my relationship with God, but now I realize that the church is within me. I thank God for stopping me in my tracks and helping me discover that I can have a deep and meaningful relationship with Him from within myself.

If God sacrificed His life for me, then why couldn't I do the same for him? These were just a few questions that I would ask myself and confront. Reflecting on the traditions and requirements of church affiliations, I realized that the deep pain within my heart was never healed unless I were to renounce it all (youth group leadership, speaking at camps as a leader, leading recovery groups, stepping away from Bible studies, and retreating from community outings). In a place called the church, God was inviting me to His intimate presence with Him on a personal level behind the scenes. I understood that we all need to be in a community setting to propel us forward in God's purpose for our lives through His will and not ours; however, I also began to understand that much of my desires were becoming intertwined with my leadership within the Church setting. Also, relying on being in fellowship with others and being part of a church to grow closer to God made me question my private relationship with God. I attended a building where it was more important to join a church with God's people so that our relationship with God could continue to thrive. I asked myself, 'Well, what if there was no one around me to keep me going to a building called a church, only to maintain some kind of relationship with God? Why did it seem that to keep my relationship with God alive, I needed to depend on my friends from church to keep me engaged? I used to be involved in so many groups in fellowship, that when I got home, I was drained from investing in relationships with others rather than with God. As I started withdrawing from the noise and chaos of society, God's Spirit of Truth was knocking at my door for a visit. As I welcomed Him into my life, His voice became powerful and clear like the roar of a lion.

He guided me into solitude to receive His teachings directly from Him. It was a humble experience, as I had to learn to be silent and listen instead of always speaking as a leader. I had to let go of my pride and ego, realizing that we are all God's children. I questioned the words I had spoken in the past, wondering if they were my own or truly from God. Now, I can reflect on moments when God's voice was silent, but now it resonates loudly within me. God tells us to come when we are ready, and I realize that I wasn't ready when I first started my Christian journey. But now, I can offer my whole self to Him in return for His offering of Himself to me.

In the realm of spirituality, it is written to present your physical forms as a living offering that is sacred and pleasing to the Divine, as this is the genuine and appropriate way to demonstrate devotion. Having been conditioned to behave in a certain manner both on and off the stage, whether in a leadership role or as part of the congregation, I began to question the established customs and circumstances of the church from a relational perspective. I can vividly recall my time as a leader in high school, witnessing other leaders encouraging the students to lift their arms in worship, to foster a deeper connection with God. Curious about the impact of this practice, I decided to inquire with some of the youth group members about their thoughts. They expressed feeling uncomfortable, uninterested, and disconnected from it. It became apparent that these were the church's established norms and traditions, aimed at conforming individuals and shaping the church environment to align with a specific standard. A standard that appeared appealing and sought-after, like being part of an exclusive group. These norms were taught within the confines of a designated place known as the 'church,' to create a more comfortable and accepting atmosphere. However, this emphasis on emotions and personal acceptance inadvertently led people astray from the true teachings and guidance of God. What happens when we leave the fervor of the church and return home, only to feel unaccepted and unwanted? Is one's relationship with our Divine Creator truly cultivated by attending these 'churches,' or is it merely a means to seek temporary emotional peace?

After spending fifteen years in a church community, I realized that I had been imitating others to fit in and feel accepted. This prevented me from having an authentic relationship with God, as I was too focused on pleasing others and avoiding rejection. Instead of offering myself as a living sacrifice to God, I was more concerned with pleasing people. I had to acknowledge that this was wrong and that my true act of worship should be focused on God, not on others. I had been driven by fear and rejection, so I immersed myself in various church ministries to find solace among others who were also broken and weary. However, I came to understand that if I truly believed in God, I needed to surrender myself to Him completely, without hesitation or regret.

In the realm of spirituality, it is emphasized that wise individuals exercise caution when it comes to speaking, and sometimes it is best to remain silent. I regret not having learned this lesson earlier in life, particularly when I assumed a leadership role at the young age of seventeen. I wish someone had advised me that developing a deep, reverent relationship with God cannot be achieved by simply attending church services, listening to a preferred pastor, or immersing oneself in church activities to the point of losing touch with God's voice calling from within. I wish I had possessed the wisdom to understand the importance of meditating on spiritual teachings day and night, seeking God earnestly, and withdrawing from the crowds to spend solitary time with Him after engaging in ministry through His guidance rather than relying solely on my strength. It is no wonder I felt exhausted and depleted. The church community was not to blame for my lack of connection with our Heavenly Father; it was my misguided habit of trying to handle everything independently for the sake of survival. The scriptures remind us, 'Come to me, all you who are weary and burdened, and I will give you rest.' God provided me with warning signs that I had strayed far from His will and become entangled in my desires.

My earthly desires were overpowering His divine presence within me. Despite the initial hardships of being led by God into solitude or a spiritual retreat, He was healing me and saving me from eternal separation from Him in Heaven. God the Father acted as both my parent and teacher, guiding me in His ways and directing me on His paths when my parents couldn't. His guidance and support provided me comfort when I strayed away from the majority. God removed me from everything I thought I knew and infused His life force into my body, mind, spirit, and soul, granting me a fresh start in life. This fresh start involved placing all my trust in Him and embracing His calling for my future. In conclusion, why would I allow any other energies to enter me, and it would cause me to stumble and fade away from what God has called me to? Such as the energy of self-pity or self-hatred, rejection, , loneliness, thoughts of suicide, anger, etc. Why would I associate with any of these energies if my God has delivered me from them all? I know my name and none of those names I identify with; therefore, I keep on pressing forward.

Chapter 9

The Raw Truth

Shortly after, I found myself in the initial stages of my spiritual journey. I realized that my connection with God was more focused on the people within the church rather than having a personal relationship with Him. I would engage in conversations about God and perform good deeds, but I lacked a genuine bond with Him. Although I would say and do things 'in the name of Jesus' and experience results, I didn't have a deep relationship with God that would secure my place in heaven. The scripture warns that many will claim to have done things in God's name, but He will turn away and say He doesn't know them. This made me question whether I was simply performing actions to earn my way into heaven or if I needed to pause and reassess my life. My relationship with God shouldn't be built solely on serving His kingdom but on the depth of my connection with Him. The scripture says, 'Confess with your mouth and BELIEVE in your heart that you MIGHT be saved.' It was easy for me to confess with my mouth, but truly believing in my heart that Jesus was my savior and Lord was a different story. Did I genuinely believe in my heart? I had heard that the heart is deceitful and filled with negative traits, as the scripture states. I knew I believed because I confessed, but the scripture also mentioned 'might be saved.' This led me to question the direction of my life and the fruit it was producing. Was I exhibiting fruit such as anger, bitterness, hatred, doubt, self-pity, and lies, which are sourced from the enemy? Or was I displaying fruit such as peace, self-control, love, goodness, patience, kindness, and joy, which are sourced from the truth (referring to the fruit of the Spirit of God rather than the fruit of the enemy or myself.)?

As I compiled those verses, I was faced with the reality of God's predetermined path for my life that resides within my control. In simpler terms, God's love for us was so immense that He sacrificed His son, allowing anyone who 'believes' to have everlasting life with Him in a realm known as Heaven, devoid of suffering, grief, and remorse. For me, it commences with 'acknowledging' and extends to 'wholeheartedly believing' that Jesus was and continues to be my guide and rescuer daily. It is a daily act of reverence, and I require considerable assistance from the genuine Counselor who has been faithfully by my side, supporting and propelling me every step of the way. This was the Divine Spirit.

 Believing in my own heart that He is the ultimate authority in my life, even when faced with financial struggles and broken relationships. Trusting in Him when others have abandoned or doubted me. Living out my faith not just in words, but in actions. Recognizing that it is the peace of God that surpasses all understanding that guides me through life's storms. Choosing to serve Him daily, seeking wisdom from others, and moving forward in unity.

Believing in Jesus as my Lord and Savior brought me to a state of humility because I felt incapable of making it on my own. I constantly felt inadequate and lacked the knowledge to navigate life. However, I experienced a spiritual awakening. God had a plan in motion, placing me on a path where I could have unwavering faith and trust in Him. I questioned who I relied on to get me through each day. If it wasn't Jesus, wouldn't I know that I am more than capable of overcoming challenges? Wouldn't I understand that God is always with me, never abandoning me, and always arriving at the perfect time? Wouldn't I know, not just feel, that He listens to my prayers and answers them? If I truly believed in my heart that Jesus is my Lord and Savior, then I would be saved. Doubt crept into my heart, leading me to examine where my loyalty truly lies: God's will or my own. By choosing to believe in my heart and mind, I found the courage to move forward and pay attention to what God was revealing to me. Many believers struggle with doubts about God's work in their lives, but God used me as an instrument to show others that there is always hope when we place our faith in our Heavenly Father.

Like the woman who had a prolonged period and was cured by her faith. Previously, she endured twelve years of being considered unclean. However, when the opportunity arose, she seized the miracle and became clean and whole due to her unwavering belief. In my own life, there have been numerous instances where I didn't receive God's blessings in my relationship because of my lack of faith. I would trust in God's ability to work miracles in other people's lives but doubted His power in my own. As time passed, I came to realize that if I am to live my life fully until my last day on Earth, I must believe that the blessings God bestows upon those He loves are also meant for me. After all, I too am a cherished child of our Heavenly Father.

Considering your faith, what are your beliefs, regardless of the situation or circumstances in your life?

The divine awakened me to fulfill my purpose. Above all, it was a renewed connection with the divine, and to spread the message that the divine is reaching out to all its children for a renewed or even a fresh connection. Recognizing that we are all united by the divine spirit, yet each person's relationship with the divine is unique, the divine still urges us to live in an authentic and sincere relationship with it.

I had two options. One was to embrace this divine calling, and the second option was to reject it. I was aware that if I chose not to accept this purpose, I would not have an eternal connection with God. I couldn't bear the thought of being one of those who claimed to have served God, only to be told that God never knew me. I couldn't risk that outcome. So, I decided to accept this calling, forsaking everything else, and took a leap of faith in writing this book. It is not just for others, but primarily for me. I want to be able to tell God, whom I wholeheartedly believe in, that I have abandoned societal norms and the ways of the world to follow and remain loyal to Him. This is what it means to be a trendsetter, rather than a follower of trends.

God had been questioning my integrity and commitment to my promises. I made a conscious decision to remain steadfast and unwavering, regardless of the circumstances around me. Previously, I built my life based on my past identities and roles, whether it was in church, home, work, or school. However, I realized that I needed to let go of those old foundations and embrace a new one. Now, my foundation is no longer unstable like sinking sand, but it is firm and solid like a rock. This foundation is rooted in the word of God and my relationship with our Heavenly Father.

Chapter 10

Now the ball's in Your court

In conclusion, I have made the conscious decision to embrace life with purpose and meaning. This purpose is to bring hope to those who have lost it and to shine light amid darkness. Throughout my journey, I realized that God had been patiently waiting for me, whispering, 'When you are ready, come to me.' It took me nearly thirty years to reach a point where I recognized the need for a personal relationship with God to guide me in the right direction, as I had reached a dead end and felt completely drained. I am incredibly grateful to embark on this adventure with our Heavenly Father here on earth, although I am aware that this is only the beginning of our deepening connection. I am no longer constrained by past obligations and the weight of titles within the confines of a church institution. Instead, I seek daily guidance and clarity through God's Word and our relationship. By living in radical faith each day, I have come to understand that living for God was His plan all along.

After wandering through what felt like a barren and exhausting desert, I finally found my home and family. The Scriptures teach us that being made in 'our image' reveals that God Himself is a community, a family. While I may not be as involved in church affiliations as before, I am now deeply connected to the source of His Word. God is and will always be my true family, for when our earthly parents forsake us, He promises to raise us. Now, my family members are God the Father, the Son, the Holy Spirit, my sister Wisdom, and my kinswoman Understanding. Seek and you shall find when you wholeheartedly seek. As I allowed God to break me down, prune away areas of my life, and rebuild me, He not only cleansed me from my dirt and impurities but also granted me a new life and a calling to live according to His will, rather than my own.

Now, I would like to invite you, as the reader, to reflect on your personal beliefs. Regardless of whether you identify as a Christian or not, do you feel like you're merely surviving each day without hope? Have past failures and doubts caused you to see yourself as just another statistic in society? Or perhaps you have everything you need and live a comfortable life. While there's nothing wrong with that, have you ever considered what comes after this life? According to the teachings, we will all face God after we pass away from this earth. Will He recognize us or turn away, saying He never knew us? It all comes down to what we truly believe in our hearts. Our beliefs shape our faith and where we place our trust. So, who or what do you put your faith in? Are you willing to make sacrifices for an eternal cause? I've discovered that having a personal relationship with our Father is crucial to avoid burnout and to stay aligned with God's calling. It's like being firmly rooted in good soil, allowing us to bear abundant and meaningful fruit. The fruit that comes from our hearts reflects what we believe. For me, I choose to believe in who God says He is, and this belief produces fruit such as love, joy, goodness, peace, mercy, and self-control. This is the kind of fruit I strive to cultivate in my life. What about your time here on Earth? Only when your earthly journey comes to an end will you face the judgment of the one true Judge? Allow me to share a glimpse of my own transformative experience in establishing a profound connection with our divine Creator. Moreover, when the time comes for your departure from this physical realm, what kind of fruit is being produced from your tree? What foundation have you chosen to anchor yourself on? Is it a solid foundation with fertile soil with rich results or a weak one that yields poor results?

In the realm of body, mind, soul, and spirit, I believe it is crucial to embrace the essence of who you truly are during your limited time to inquire about your spiritual journey, you cannot claim that no one ever inquired, for I am doing so now. I intend to pass on the wisdom and insights I have acquired and continue to acquire, regarding nurturing a personal relationship with our heavenly Father. What will you do with your relationship with our Creator, starting now?

The ball is in your court. It's your turn now. Ready, set, go!

9 789655 786682